Wacky World of...
Inexplicable Inventions!

by
Hermione Redshaw

BEARPORT
PUBLISHING

Minneapolis, Minnesota

CREDITS

All images are courtesy of Shutterstock.com, unless otherwise specified. With thanks to Getty Images, Thinkstock Photo, and iStockphoto.

Recurring assets – Lelene (header font), MaryMB (explosion), RoyaltyFreeStockVectors (spiral), Ardea, hvostik (series logo), Amy Li (additional illustrations). Cover – HomeArt, Alexander Konradi, p2–3 – Sunny studio, p4–5 – FG Trade, EdgarMueller, Marharyta Gangalo, Hafiez Razali, kkbs1707, izusek, p6–7 – berkut, Kwangmoozaa, p8–9 – Elenia Photo, Nils Jacobi, p10–11 – wavebreakmedia, TashaNatasha, vectorplus, Worrawoot.s, Blue Planet Studio, p12–13 – 279photo, Natalia Tiabina, p14–15 – aquariagirl1970, LightField Studios, p16–17 – DenisNata, Nadiia Korol, Shadow Inspiration, SvetlanaFedoseyeva, EkaterinaDanilova, izusek, p18–19 – haryigit, p20–21 – Alexander Konradi, Anatolir, g_tech, huntingSHARK, Pavel K, vladwel, p22–23 – Olga1818, xiaorui, Mega Pixel, Koltsov.

Library of Congress Cataloging-in-Publication Data is available at www.loc.gov or upon request from the publisher.

ISBN: 979-8-88509-382-8 (hardcover)
ISBN: 979-8-88509-504-4 (paperback)
ISBN: 979-8-88509-619-5 (ebook)

© 2023 Booklife Publishing
This edition is published by arrangement with Booklife Publishing.

North American adaptations © 2023 Bearport Publishing Company. All rights reserved. No part of this publication may be reproduced in whole or in part, stored in any retrieval system, or transmitted in any form or by any means, electronic, mechanical, photocopying, recording, or otherwise, without written permission from the publisher.

For more information, write to Bearport Publishing, 5357 Penn Avenue South, Minneapolis, MN 55419.

CONTENTS

INVENTIONS. 4
AIR-CONDITIONED JACKET 6
PET UMBRELLA 8
PAMPER YOUR PET 10
CUBE WATERMELONS 12
MILK CLOTHES. 14
FOOD FASHION. 16
POTATO BATTERY 18
IMPROBABLE INVENTIONS. . . . 22
GLOSSARY. 24
INDEX 24

INVENTIONS

There is no doubt that humans do some very strange things. We chalk holes to other worlds in the sidewalk and shape houses out of clay. Some people have even spent a year in bed . . . for science!

Some of our craziest ideas come as we try to solve a problem (sometimes before one even exists). Inventions can be interesting, imaginative, and even **inexplicable**. Let's learn about some of the wildest and wackiest things people have made!

AIR-CONDITIONED JACKET

If you're hot why not grab a jacket? This jacket is unlike any other—one that has air-conditioning built into it. The idea started in Japan when creator Hiroshi Ichigaya wanted to **design** an air conditioner that didn't use much power.

Air-conditioning can cool down air if you feel too hot.

With cooling jackets, you don't need to cool an entire room to stay comfortable. You just have to zip up your jacket! This cool clothing was put to the test in 2011 when an earthquake and tsunami knocked out power in Japan. And it worked!

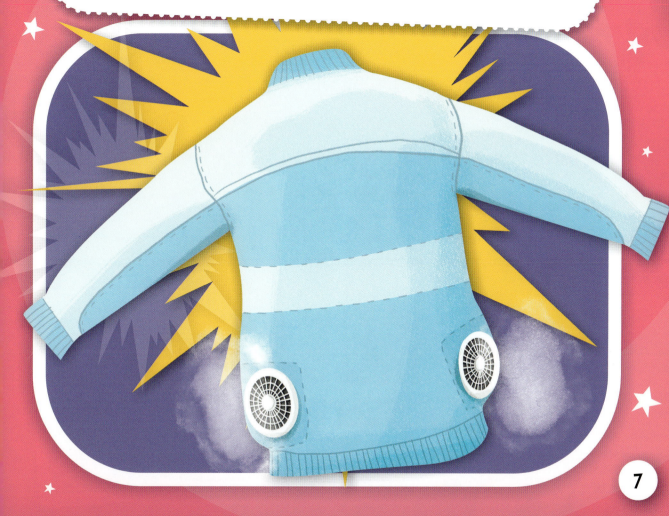

PET UMBRELLA

It's not just humans that use incredible inventions. So do our pets! There are fancy feeding systems and coats to keep them warm. There are even umbrellas for pets.

Would you give your cat a coat?

Pet umbrellas are designed to work just like umbrellas for humans. Some pet umbrellas are attached to leashes. Others hook to pet coats, collars, or harnesses.

A PET UMBRELLA KEEPS YOUR POOCH DRY DURING A WALK IN THE RAIN.

PAMPER YOUR PET

When it comes to making things for our pets, the list of inexplicable inventions is endless.

A self-cleaning litter box.

A ball **launcher** that plays catch with your dog.

A fish wheelchair!

What would you want to invent for your pet?

You'll need to think about a few things . . .
- What does your pet invention do?
- What is it called?
- What could you do to make it even more amazing?

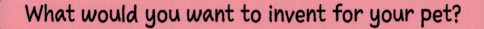

PITCH YOUR INVENTION TO A FRIEND. THIS IS WHEN YOU EXPLAIN WHAT YOUR INVENTION DOES AND WHY IT IS SO GREAT.

CUBE WATERMELONS

Humans are always inventing ways to change the shape of food. Sometimes, we make our food look nice when we put it on a plate. Other times, we change the way it grows!

Cube watermelons were invented by Tomoyuki Ono.

Cube watermelons are grown in boxes with strong, straight sides. Why do the boxes need to be strong? Because these fruits are tough and could break weak growing boxes.

MILK CLOTHES

Food inventions may be fun to eat. But they can also be good to wear. Materials company Mi Terro turned a glass of milk into a T-shirt!

Turning milk into clothes takes around two months. One glass of milk can make five shirts!

We've learned how to make clothes out of milk that is no longer okay to drink. This is known as **upcycling**. Clothing companies are starting to use this **eco-friendly** fabric option.

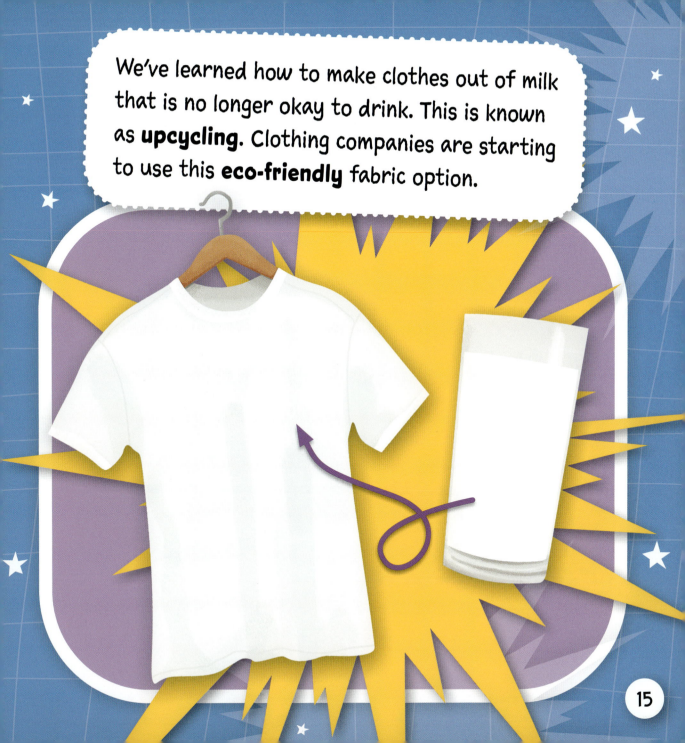

FOOD FASHION

Do you have any favorite foods that might be fun to wear?

Maybe you've always wanted chocolate shoes, strawberry earrings, or an outfit made of lettuce.

Design your own food clothes. Think about . . .

What event would you wear the clothes to?

Is the outfit fancy or casual?

Who might want to wear it?

What else could you wear with the clothing?

POTATO BATTERY

Food can be so many things. In fact, did you know that a potato can be a battery? Humans are always looking for new types of power that are better for the planet. Potatoes might be the next big thing!

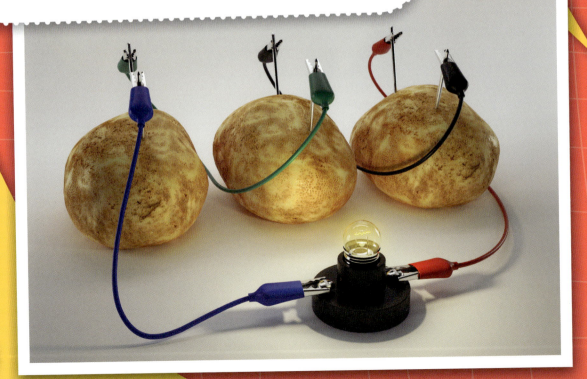

Potatoes can create power when mixed with metals. You would need a lot of them to power something as big as your television. But with a couple of potatoes, you can power a small light.

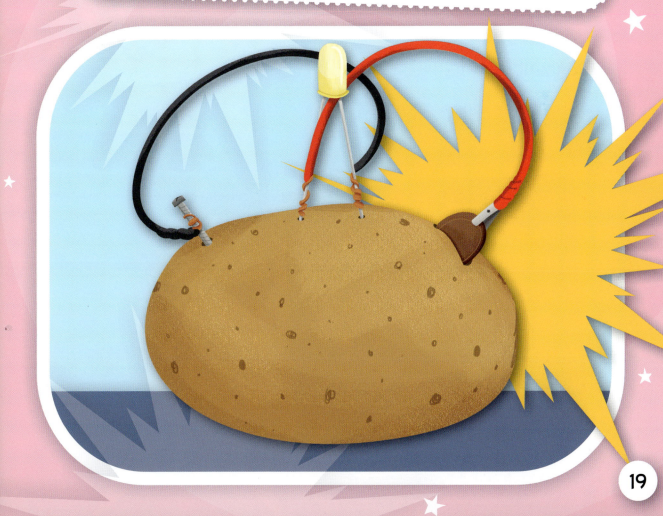

Make your own potato battery. First, grab:
- Potatoes
- Copper coins
- Silver coins
- Wires with crocodile clips
- A small **LED** light

Crocodile clips

You can also try other foods to see what else could be a battery.

1. Push one copper coin and one silver coin into your potato.

2. Connect one crocodile clip from your copper coin to the light bulb.

YOU MAY NEED MORE THAN ONE POTATO. CONNECT THE POTATOES TOGETHER WITH CROCODILE CLIPS FROM SILVER COINS TO COPPER COINS.

3. Connect another crocodile clip from your silver coin to the light.

4. Does your bulb light up?

IMPROBABLE INVENTIONS

Check out even more silly inventions!

BABY MOP
- Made in 2012
- Baby clothes that clean the floor while the baby crawls around

AUTOMATIC CLOTHES FOLDER
- Made in 2019
- A machine that folds your clothes for you

SELFIE TOASTER
- Made in 2014
- Cooks your face on toast

The next time you have a problem, think of an invention to solve it. Even the inexplicable can be brought to life.

GLOSSARY

cube a shape with six square sides

design to think up, plan, or create

eco-friendly something that's not harmful to Earth or the environment

inexplicable extremely odd or difficult to explain

launcher something that sends an object forward

LED an energy-efficient way of producing light

upcycling making something old into something new

INDEX

air-conditioning 6
batteries 18, 20
clothes 7, 14-15, 17, 22
designing 6, 9, 17
food 12, 14, 16-18, 20
milk 14-15
pets 8-11
potatoes 18-21
watermelon 12-13